INTERNATIONAL ANNUAL
FLORAL ART 06/07

stichting kunstboek

Every year the International Annual of Floral Art makes a round-up
of what lives among creative people all over the world who use flowers
and vegetal elements as a form of expression. Compared to last year
we have noted that the floral world has changed rapidly. Cheap flights,
international demonstrations, magazines and books, Internet communication …
they all make it possible to be informed about new trends in no time.
Very striking this year is the enormous boost of the floral expression in Eastern
Europe, with Russia in the lead. That's why our international jury encouraged
Zhanna Semenova, and with her 'the Russian school', with the Bronze Leaf.
The Golden Leaf went to the work of Yuko Takagi from Japan, while Rob Plattel
from the Netherlands received the Silver Leaf.
From the 886 submissions, 251 were retained and depicted in this year's edition.
When making the selection, the jury kept our aim in mind, which was to give
a platform to the international floral art and to stimulate an interchange
of inspiration in the floral world.

I'd like to especially thank our international jury, who invested their time
and their expert knowledge in order to select the best works and the
strongest personalities.

And last but certainly not least, I would like to thank all florists for the
energy they've invested in their submissions. Those efforts make this book
so unique in the floral world: it's the sum of an enormous amount of energy,
which turns every creation into a personal piece of art. And this shows
in every page of this reference work.
Discover and enjoy!

Jaak Van Damme
Publisher

Mark Van Berckelaer
France

During the years following his floristic training in the 1960s, Mark Van Berckelaar had the opportunity to do a number of interesting internships at famous houses like Isabelle De Backer in Brussels (currently Daniël Ost). Afterwards he started his own business in Antwerp.

He was the technical organizer of the European Cup in 1983, which led to numerous contacts with foreign top florists. Afterwards he has worked closely together with many of them, but especially with his friend Daniël Ost.

After years of giving demonstrations abroad (Taiwan, Japan, China and most European countries) he became the general director of Floral Art at Formafleur, France's most important training centre for florists.

Moniek Vanden Berghe
Belgium

After her training in painting, ceramics and sculpting and after gaining a couple of years of working experience as a graphic designer, Moniek Vanden Berghe has focused on floral art. She's currently known all over the world, especially for her innovative bridal work. She has been a teacher at the Florademie in Sint-Truiden, is guest lecturer at various training institutes in Belgium and abroad and gives demonstrations in Belgium, the Netherlands, France, Scotland, Japan, USA ...

In Cleome, her own flower shop/school, she gives workshops and lessons to both experts and amateurs. Moniek also designs floristic recipients and dresses stands and showrooms for companies. After having participated in the publications: *Masters of flower arrangements* (Stichting Kunstboek, 1993), *Floral Masterpieces of Belgium* (Stichting Kunstboek, 1996) and *World flower artists* (Thalacker medien, 1999), she has published her own successful book *Flowers in Love* (Stichting Kunstboek, 2005).

Guido Müskens
The Netherlands

Guido Müskens took Professional training in Nijmegen and Master's training in Utrecht and afterwards also took a Teacher training in 's-Hertogenbosch. Nowadays he teaches Master classes at Helicon Opleidingen MBO 's-Hertogenbosch, where he is also team leader of the teachers' group. He gives demonstrations in the Netherlands and abroad.

Bea Beroy i Villacampa
Spain

After having finished her agricultural engineer studies at the Universidad de Barcelona, Bea Beroy i Villacampa became Oficial Florista i Especialización at the Escola d'Art Floral de Catalunya, qualified by the INCANOP and the FEEF. She then took a teachers' training course at the Departamento de Treball of the Generalitat de Catalunya, followed by specialization courses with the teachers of the Escola (like Llum Benedicto, Montserrat Bolet, Alfons Tost) and with the European teachers Gregor Lersch, Peter Hess, Marie Bosson, Wally Klett and Enrique León. She continued her teachers' training in floral art at the Floristik Britta Ohlrogge and Daniel Santamaria in Hamburg and at the Escola in Catalunya, where she has taught since 1994.

Nowadays she gives expositions and exhibitions in companies and organisations in the floral sector. She has been a jury member in several international competitions and was assistant at the team of the Interflora Cup in 1991, the Cup of Spain in 1994 and the Europe Cup in 1999. In 2003 she was a jury member at the Europe Cup.

JOUNI SEPPÄNEN
Finland

Jouni Seppänen is one of the leading master florists in Europe today. In addition to having won the Finnish Championships six times, he has received many awards and honours in Finland and abroad. His large flower shop, situated in the city centre of his home town Helsinki, specializes in floral arrangements for business clients and harbours a large orchid collection. Jouni also travels around the world giving workshops, seminars and demonstrations. His latest passions are his arrangements for Flower and Fashion Shows. In his own country he was the instigator for the start of master florist education. Furthermore he was called upon by the Ministry of Education to create the new forms of florist and master florist degrees. Next to all these activities, Jouni also has his own education and consulting company HANA Floral Art Institute.

Roser Bofill i Soliguer
Spain

Roser Bofill I Soliguer is co-founder and current director of the Escola d'Art Floral de Catalunya, chairwoman of the Associació Catalana d'Escoles d'Art Floral i Jardinería and member of both the CHOC and the Spanish commission of education of the FEEF. She became a Master in History of Art at the Universidad de Barcelona and qualified in interior design at the Escola Eina de Barcelona. Afterwards she took teachers' training courses at the Departamento de Treball of the Generalitat de Cataluyna and specialization courses with European teachers like Gregor Lersch, Paul and Ursula Wegener, Peter Hess, Jean-Marie Leemans, Wally Klett, Nicole von Boletzky, Olaf Schroers and Enrique León. She also took teachers' training courses in floral art at the Atelier 5 of Basilea, the Weihenstephan of Freising, the Floristik Britta Ohlrogge and Daniel Santamaria in Hamburg and at the Escola in Catalunya, where she now teaches. Her specialization is the history of art and the theory of floral art.

THE JURY

GOLDEN LEAF

Yuko TAKAGI

Japan

Yuko TAKAGI
Japan

Yuko TAKAGI

Japan

SILVER LEAF

Rob PLATTEL
The Netherlands

Rob PLATTEL
The Netherlands

Rob PLATTEL
The Netherlands

BRONZE LEAF

Zhanna SEMENOVA

Russia

Zhanna SEMENOVA
Russia

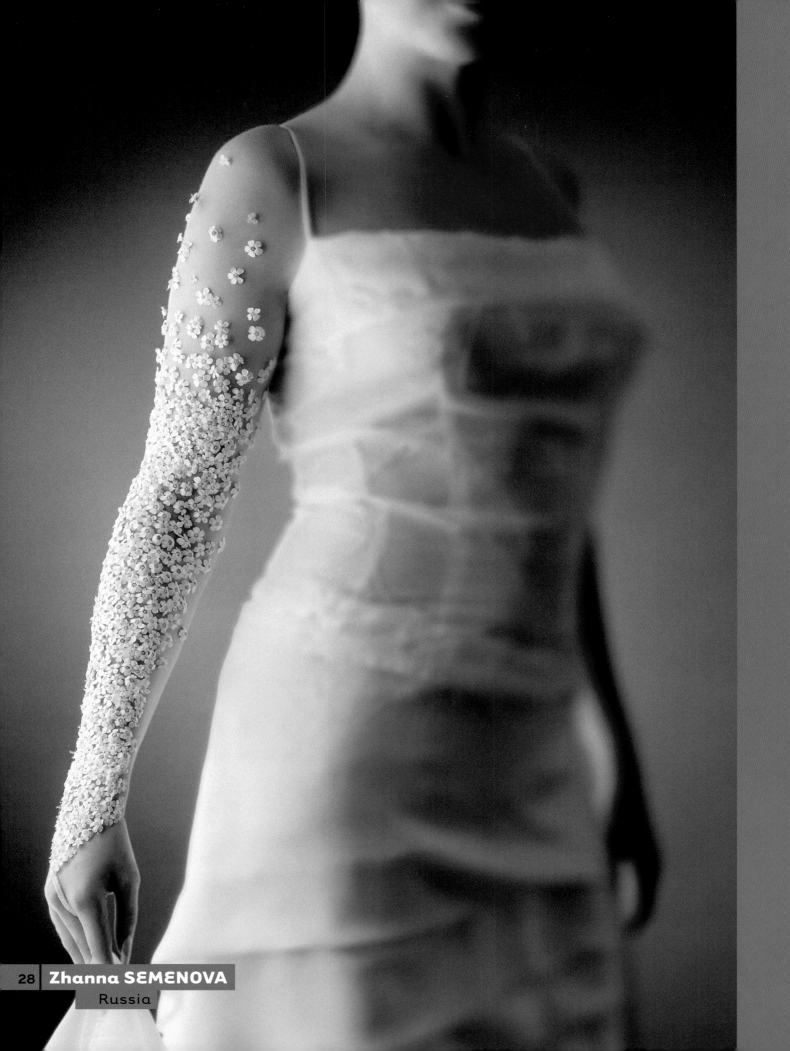

Zhanna SEMENOVA
Russia

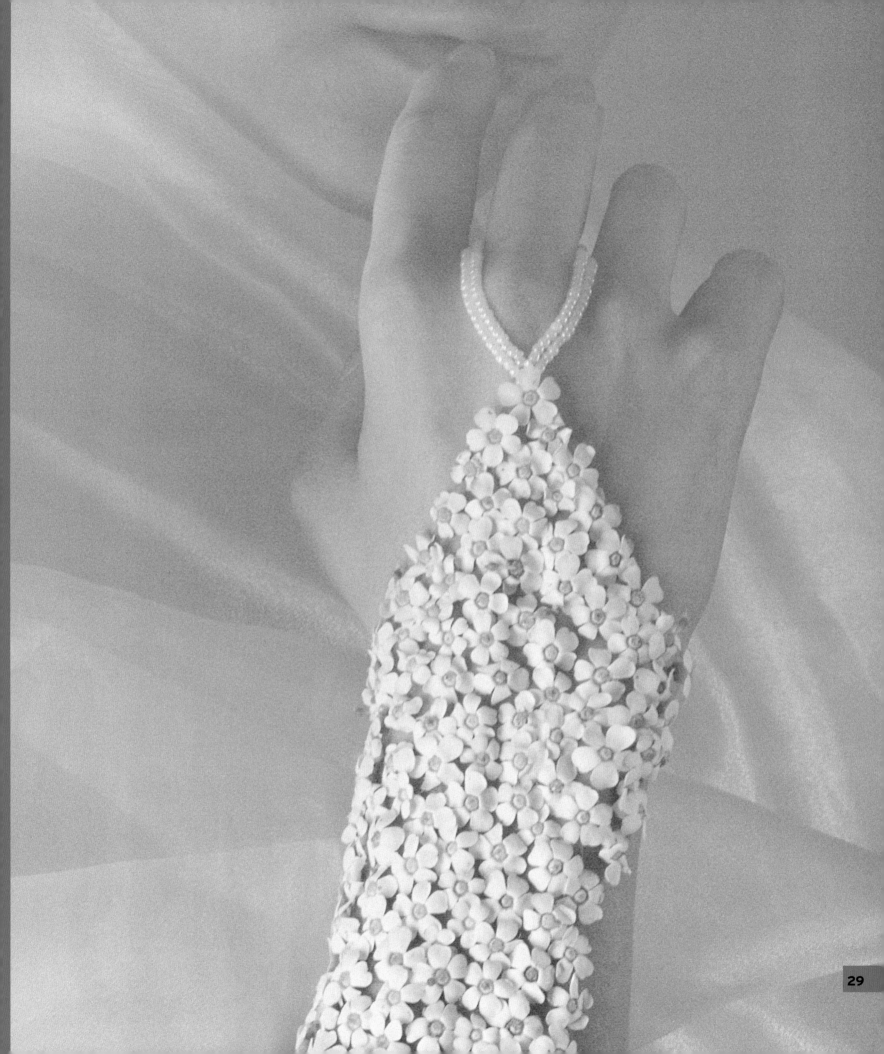

SELECTION

Jean-Louis AMICE
France

Ingeborg AUGUSTUS
Belgium

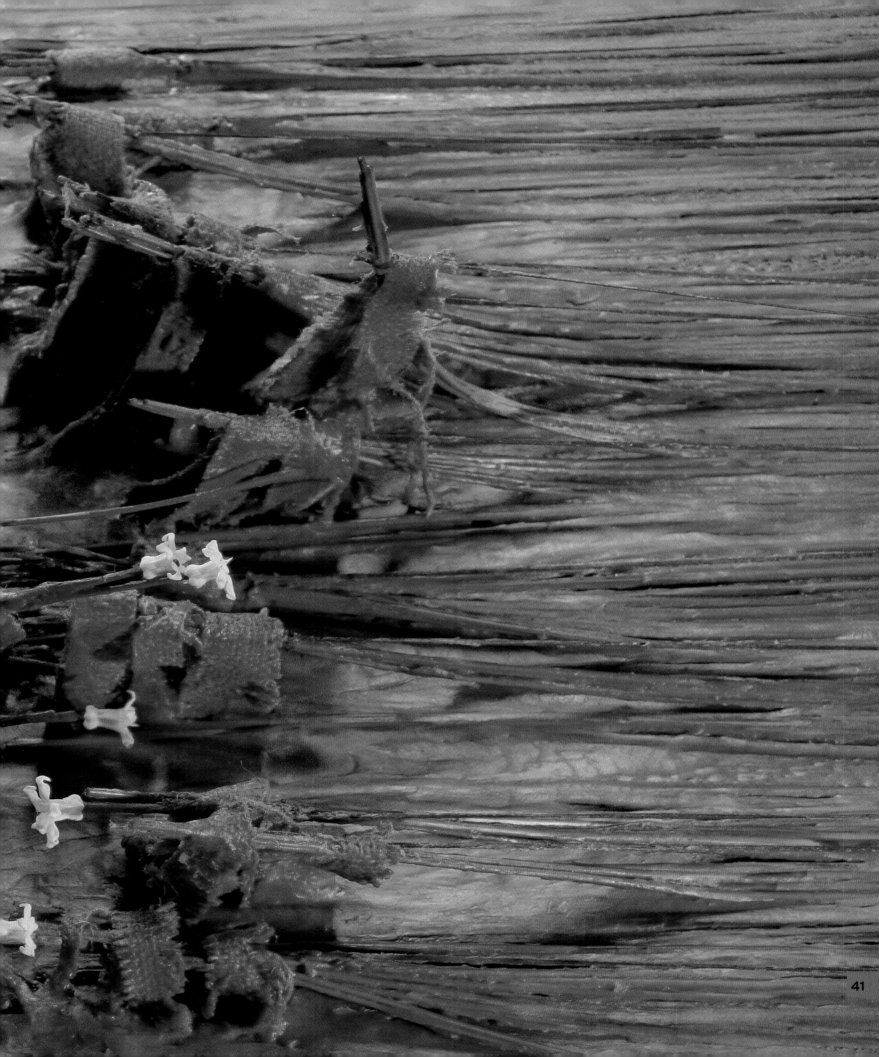

Per BENJAMIN
Sweden

Alexander BERMIJAKOV
Russia

Montse BOLET I SOLER
Spain

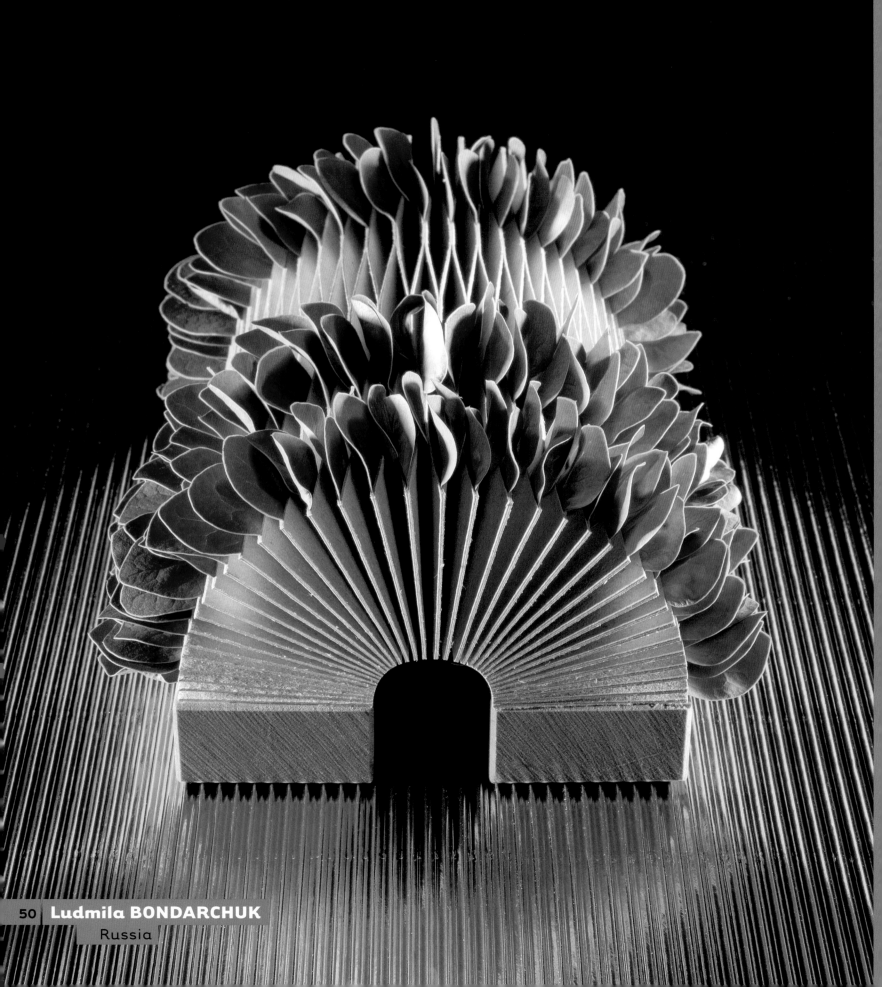

Ludmila BONDARCHUK
Russia

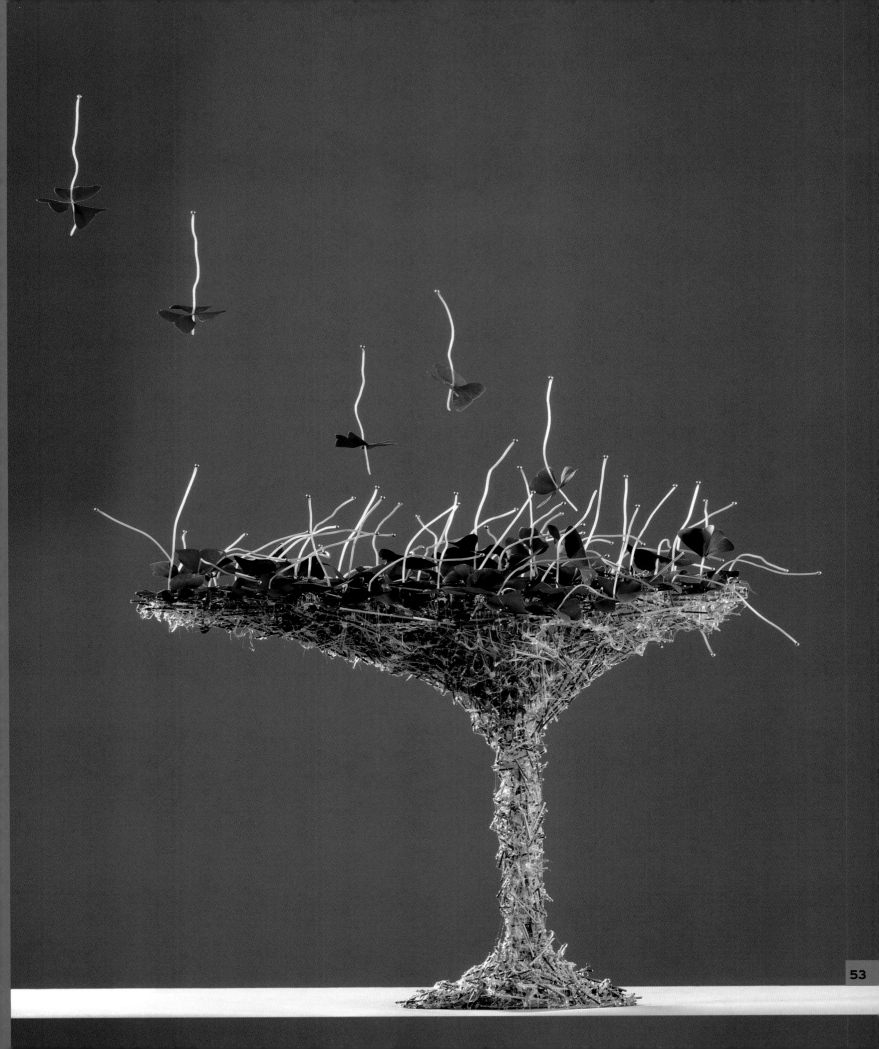

Alexey BULATOV
Russia

Lorna CAMPBELL
United Kingdom

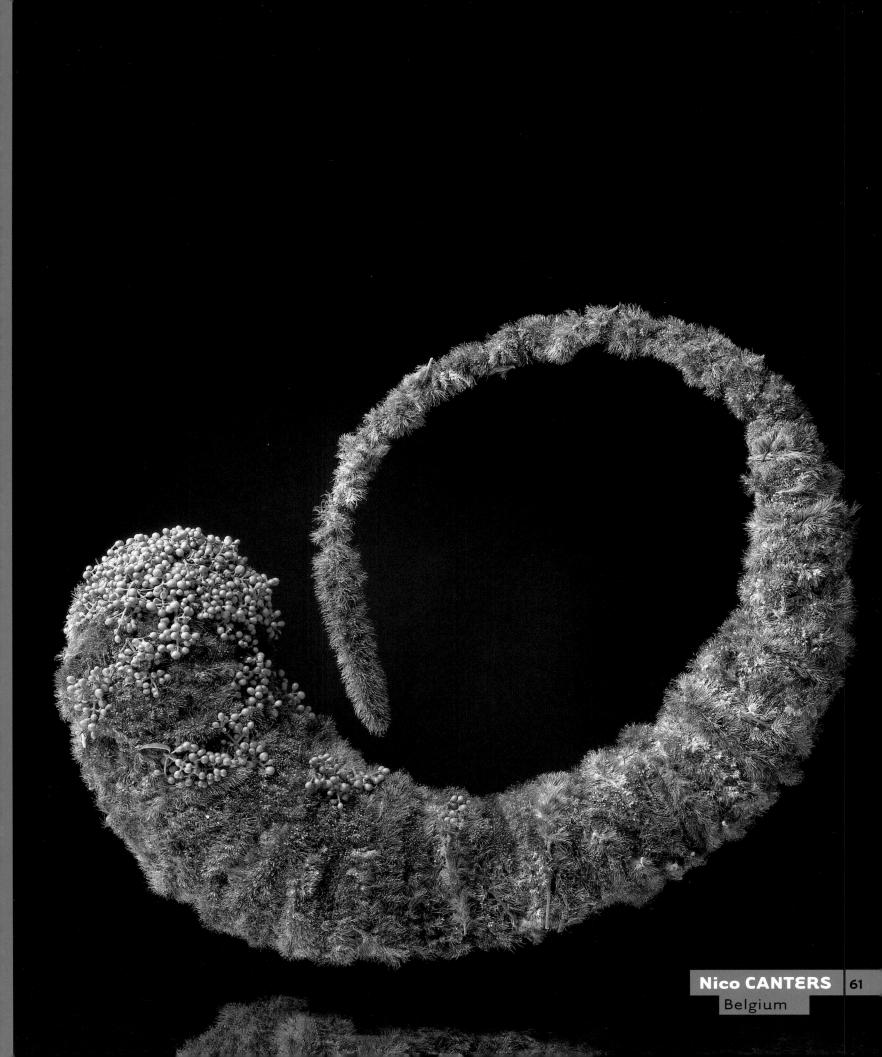

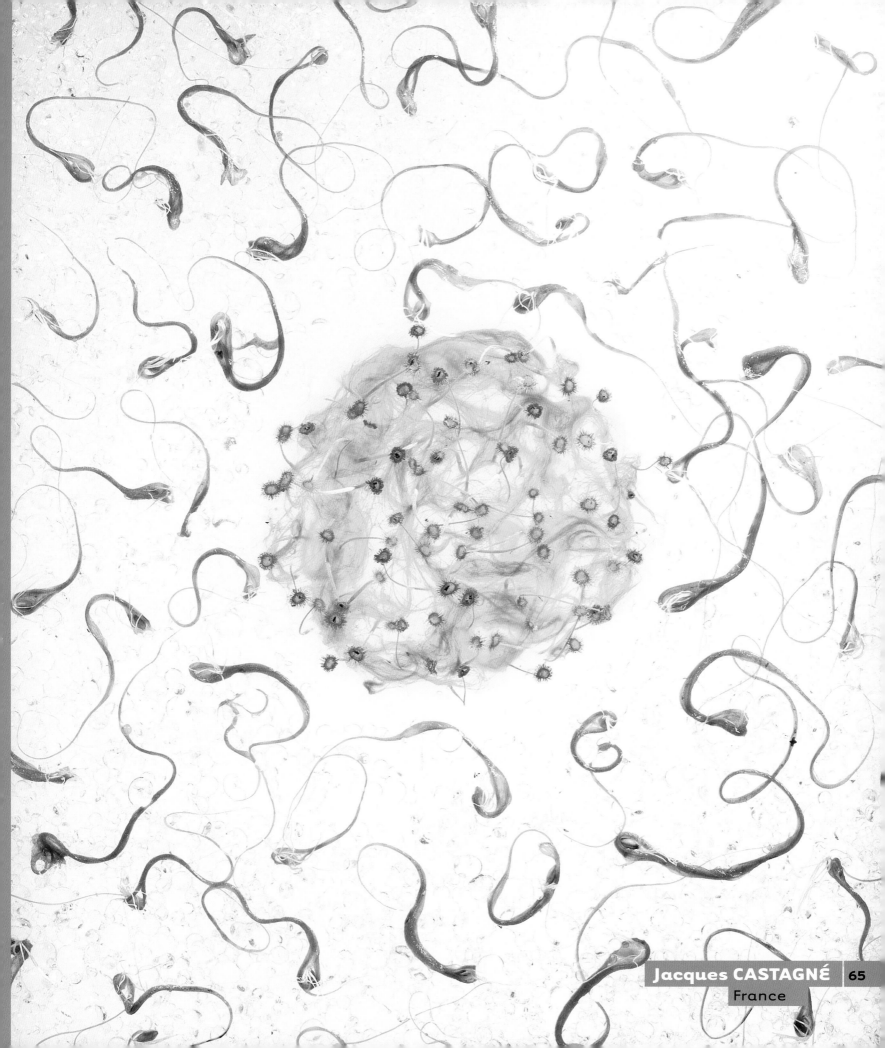

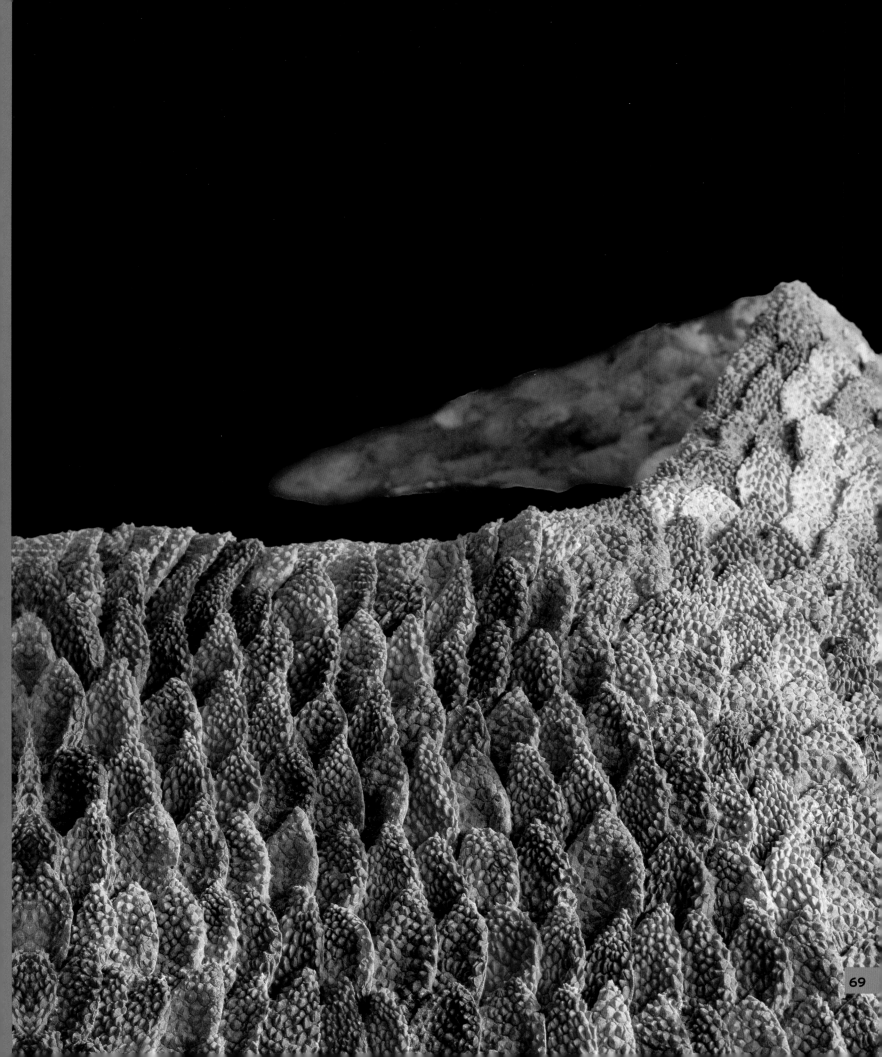

Maria DE LA LUZ REYES CAMACHO
Spain

Gudrun COTTENIER
Belgium

Tomas DE BRUYNE
Belgium

Kristof DE WAELE
Belgium

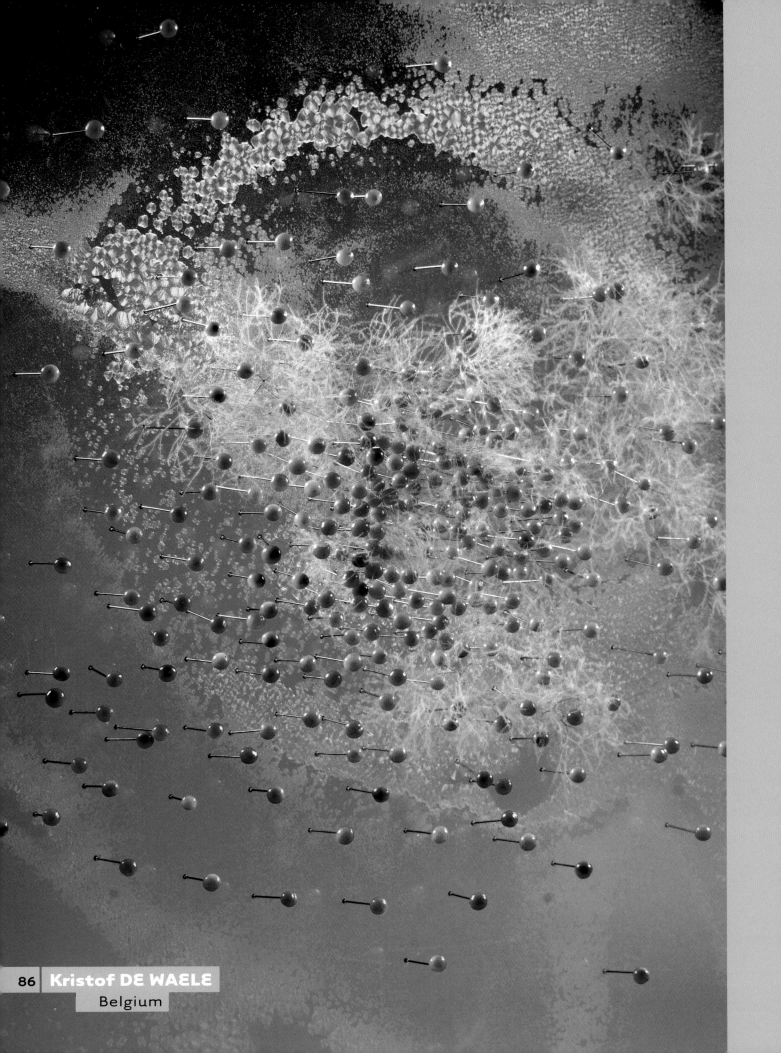

Kristof DE WAELE
Belgium

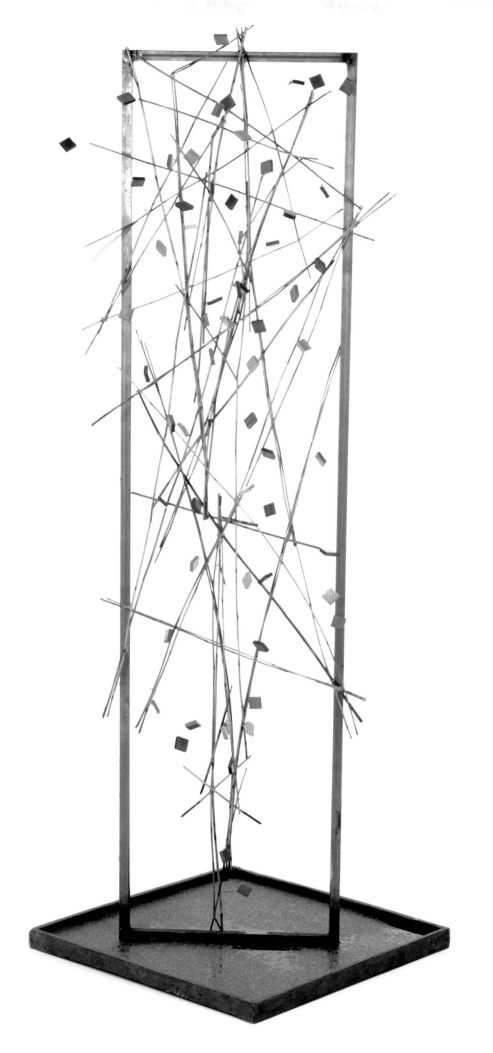

André DIERICKX
Belgium

André DIERICKX
Belgium

Araik GALSTYAN
Armenia

Lien GELLYNCK
Belgium

Richard GO
Australia

Rita GYBELS
Belgium

Rita GYBELS
Belgium

Karin HERGEMÖLLER
Germany

Annemie KANTERS-BEELEN
The Netherlands

Sergey KARPUNIN
Russia

Wally KLETT
Germany

Sabine KLOOSTERMAN-CALAME
Canada

Robert KOENE
Greece

Patrick KOKINOPOULOS
France

Elena KUPRINA
Russia

Natalia KORYAKINA
Russia

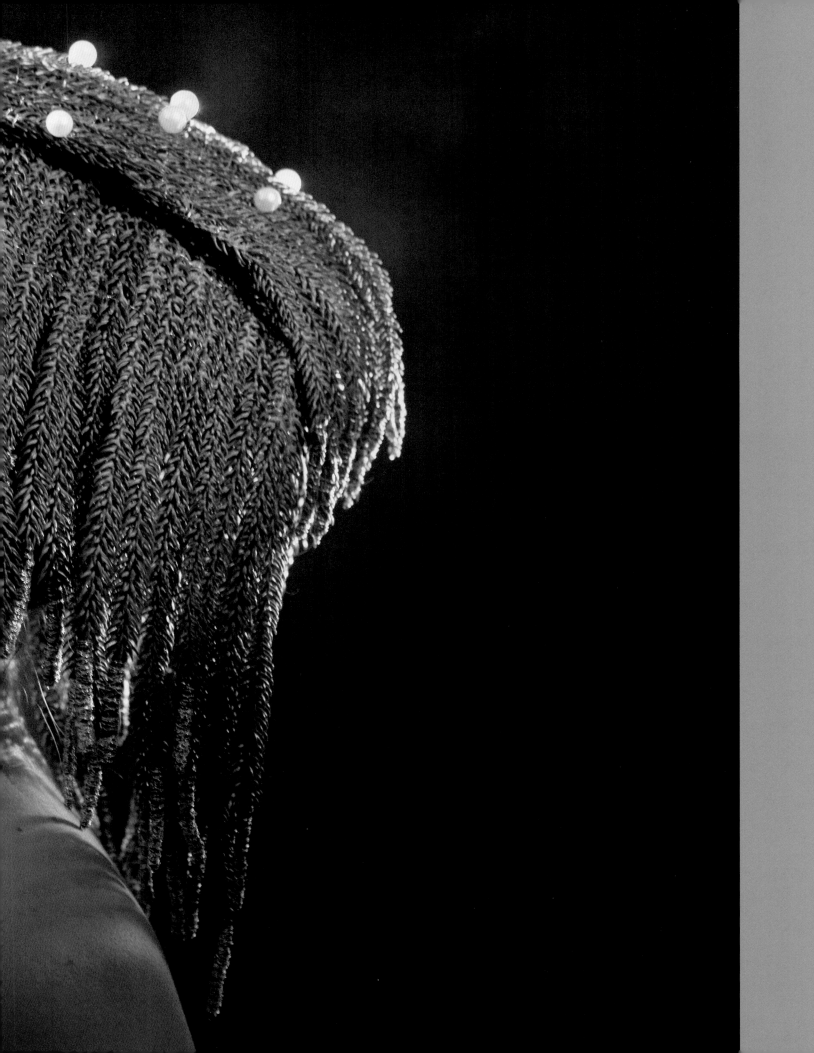

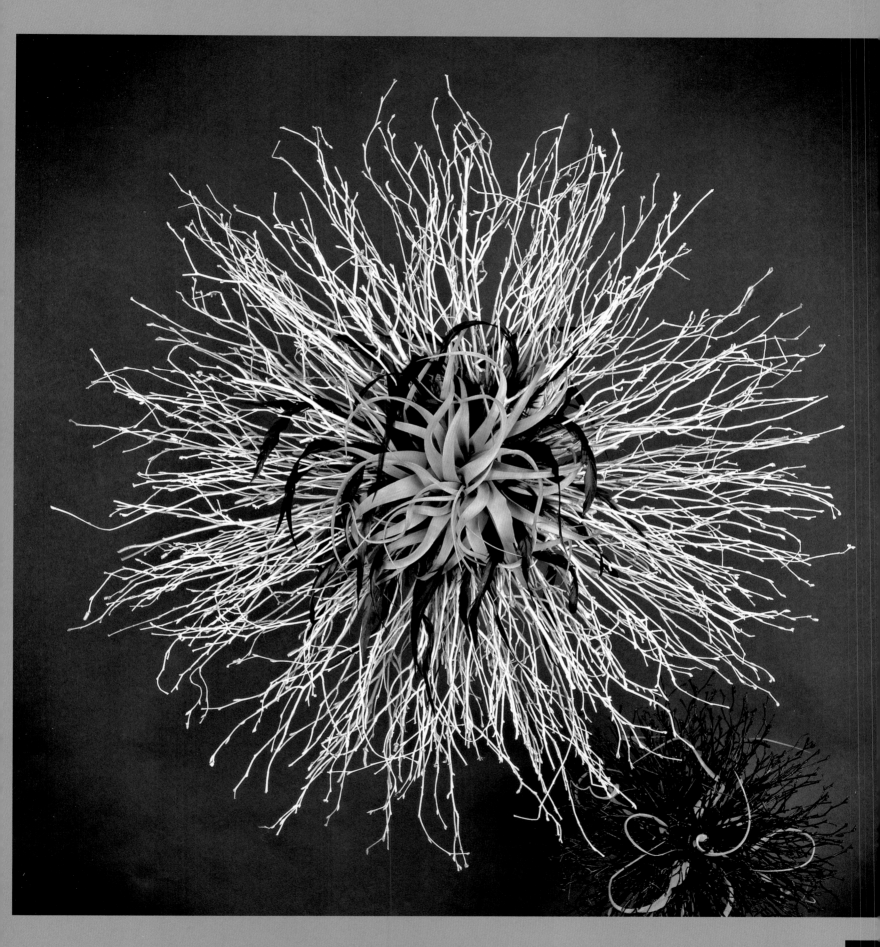

Konstantin LAZAREV
Russia

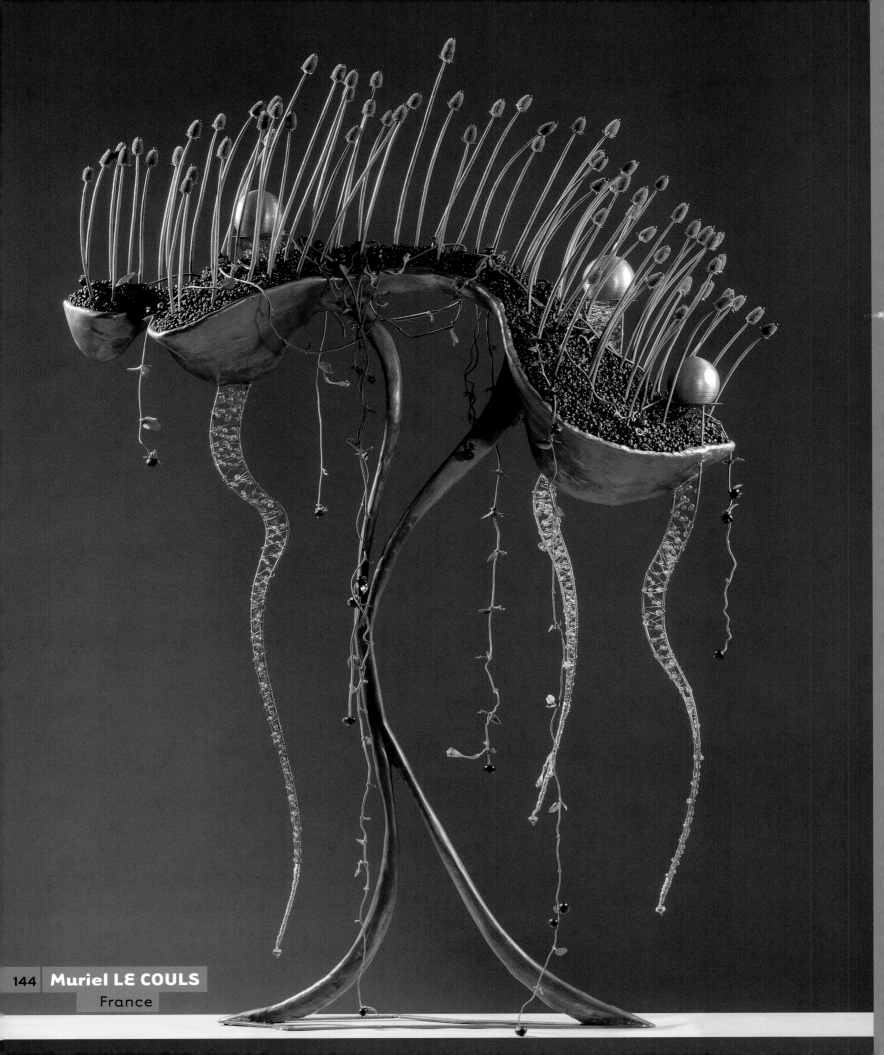

Muriel LE COULS
France

Arnaud LECHANTRE
France

Anson LOW
Singapore

Svetlana METALNIKOVA
Russia

Svetlana METALNIKOVA
Russia

Allysha HUETER
Australia

Holly MONEY–COLLINS
USA

Guido MÜSKENS
The Netherlands

Yukiko NISHIMURA
Japan

Hiroyuki OKA

Japan

Hiroyuki OKA
Japan

Erika OLDENHOF
The Netherlands

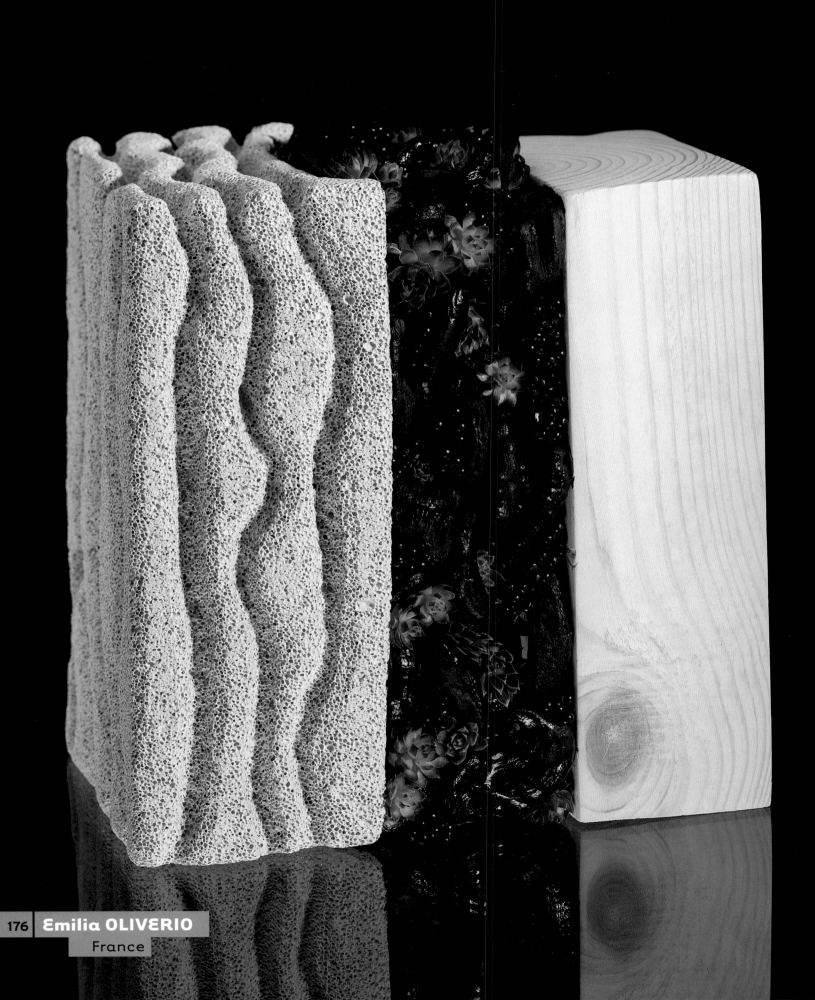

Emilia OLIVERIO
France

Jin-Young PARK
Korea

Mark PAMPLING
Australia

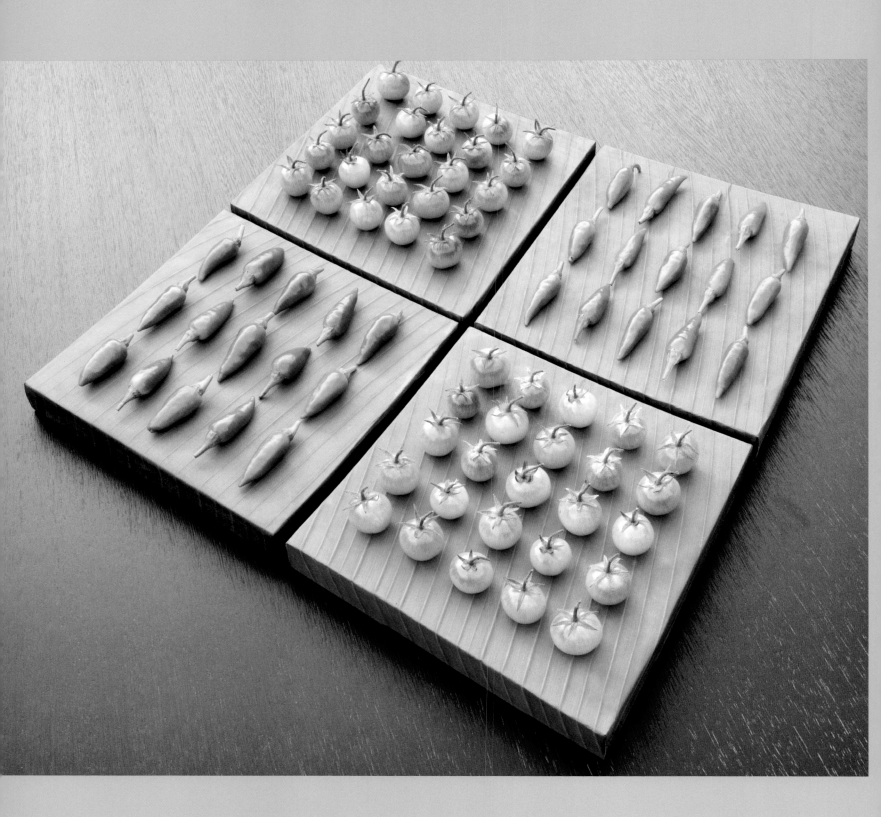

Salvatore PAPARELLA
Italy

Geert PATTYN

Belgium

Geert PATTYN
Belgium

Kristel REMIJN

The Netherlands

Stefan ROOSEN
Belgium

Veaceslav ROSCA
Russia

Naoki SASAKI
Japan

Ute SCHMIDT
Germany

Jouni SEPPÄNEN
Finland

Jouni SEPPÄNEN
Finland

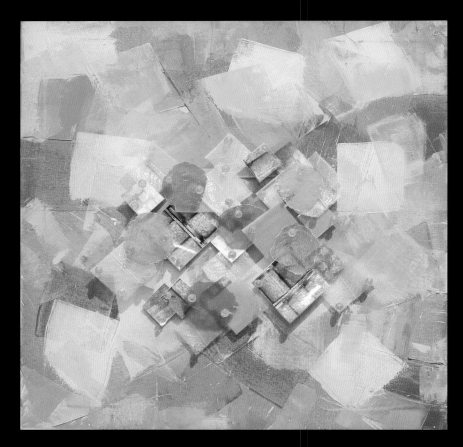

Sveta SHVEDENKOVA
Russia

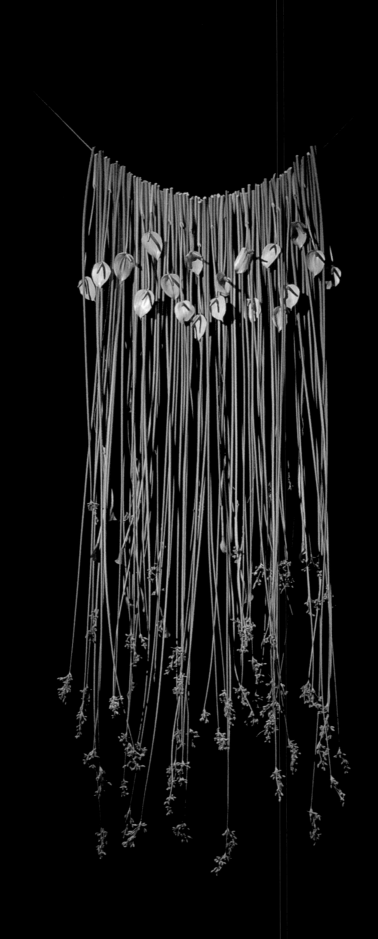

Giordano SIMONELLI
Italy

Britta SPELLEKEN
Germany

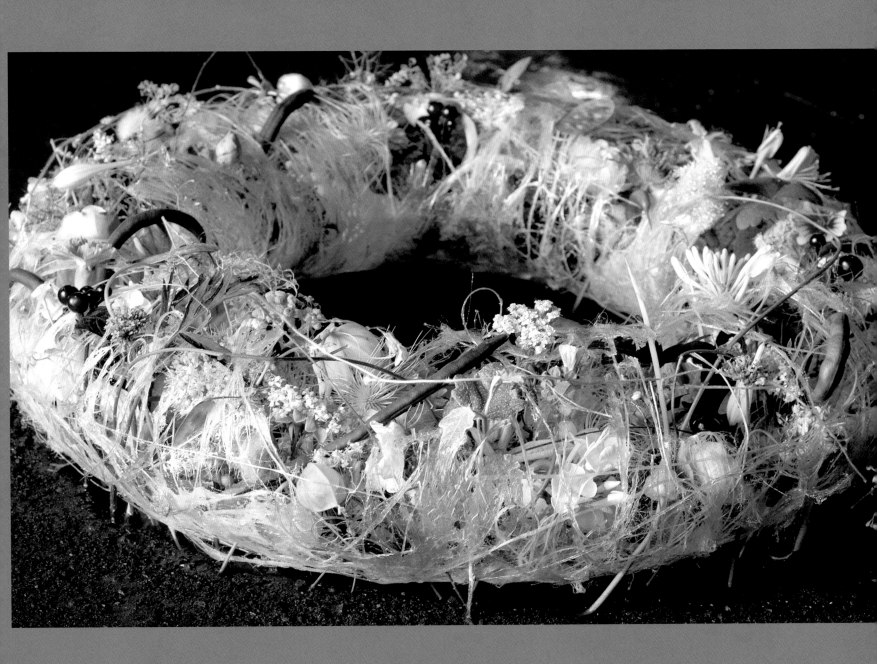

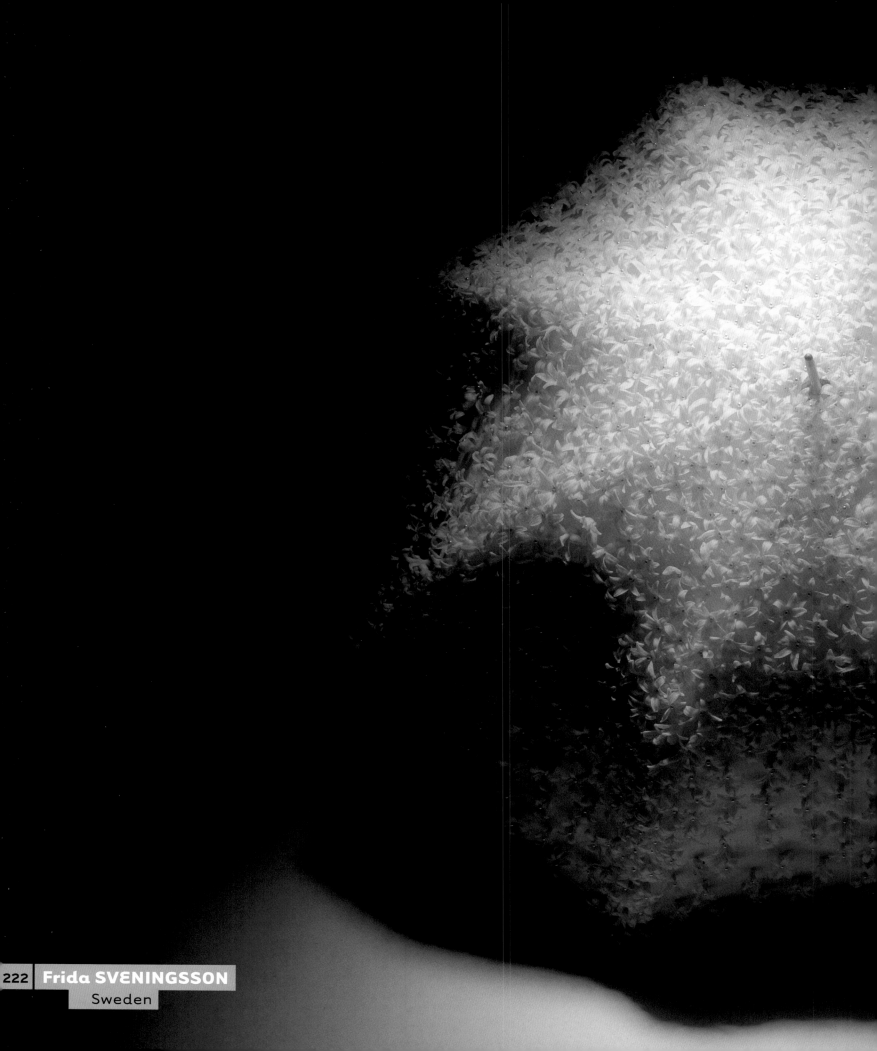

Frida SVENINGSSON
Sweden

June TAN
Singapore

Tracy TOMLINSON
United Kingdom

Tatjana TRIDVORNOVA
Estonia

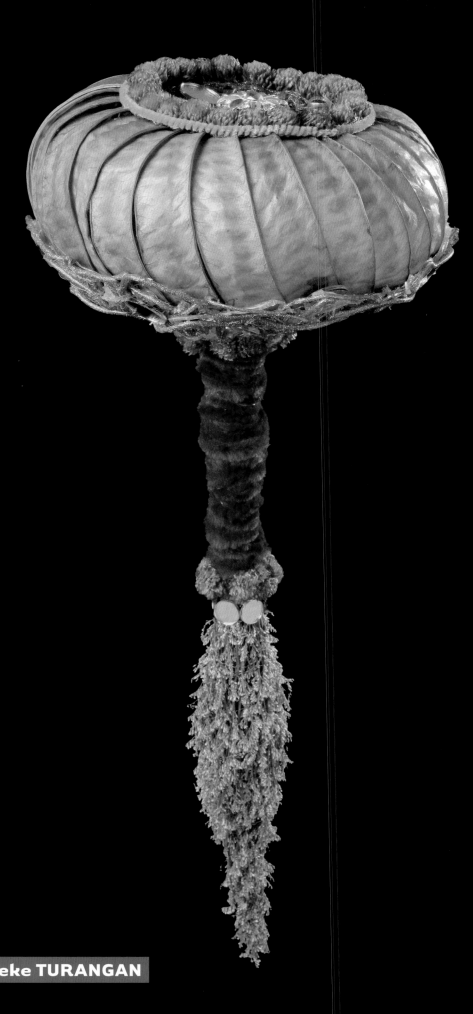

Teresa Maria Ineke TURANGAN
Indonesia

Andy Djati UTOMO
Indonesia

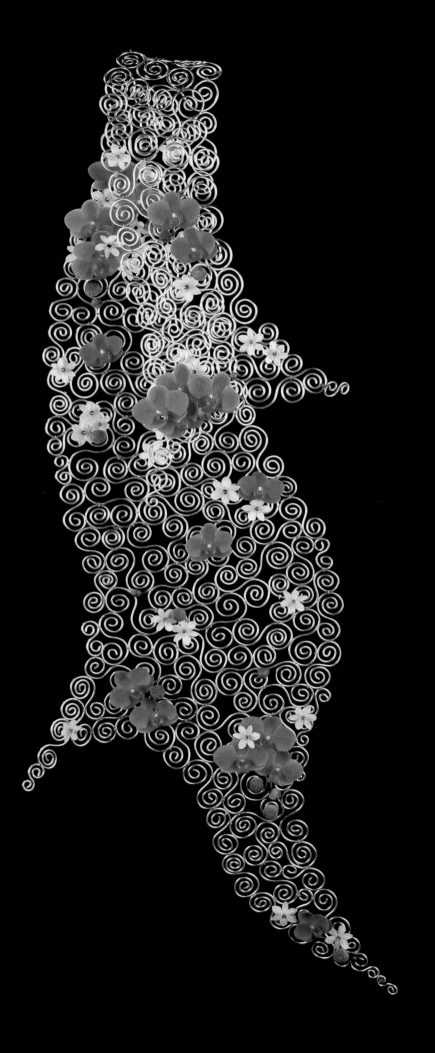

Mark VAN BERCKELAER
France

Mark VAN BERCKELAER
France

Moniek VANDEN BERGHE
Belgium

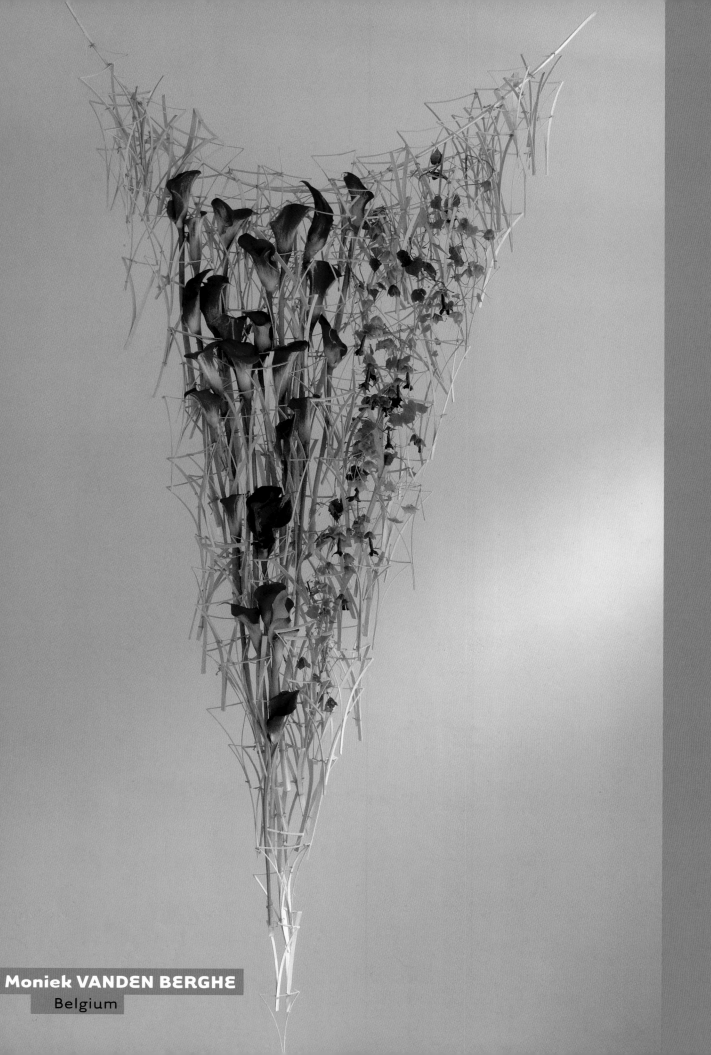

Moniek VANDEN BERGHE
Belgium

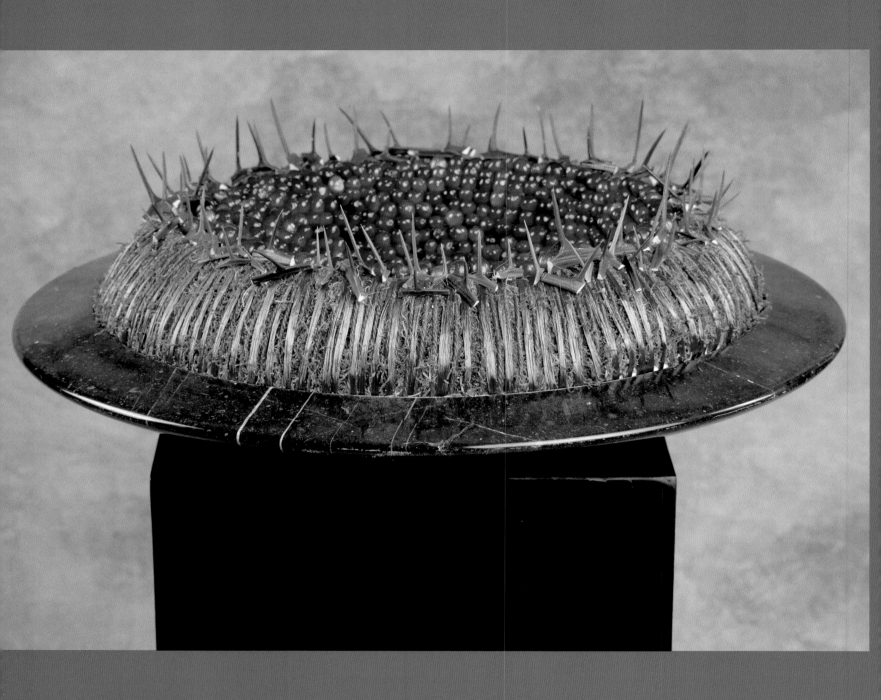

Marion VAN DER VEEN
The Netherlands

Max VAN DE SLUIS
The Netherlands

Marcel VAN DIJK

The Netherlands

Marcel VAN DIJK
The Netherlands

Herman VAN DIONANT
Belgium

Françoise VANDONINK
Belgium

Annick VAN WESEMAEL
Belgium

Annick VAN WESEMAEL
Belgium

Kristin VORELAND
Norway

Jessica WAHL
Sweden

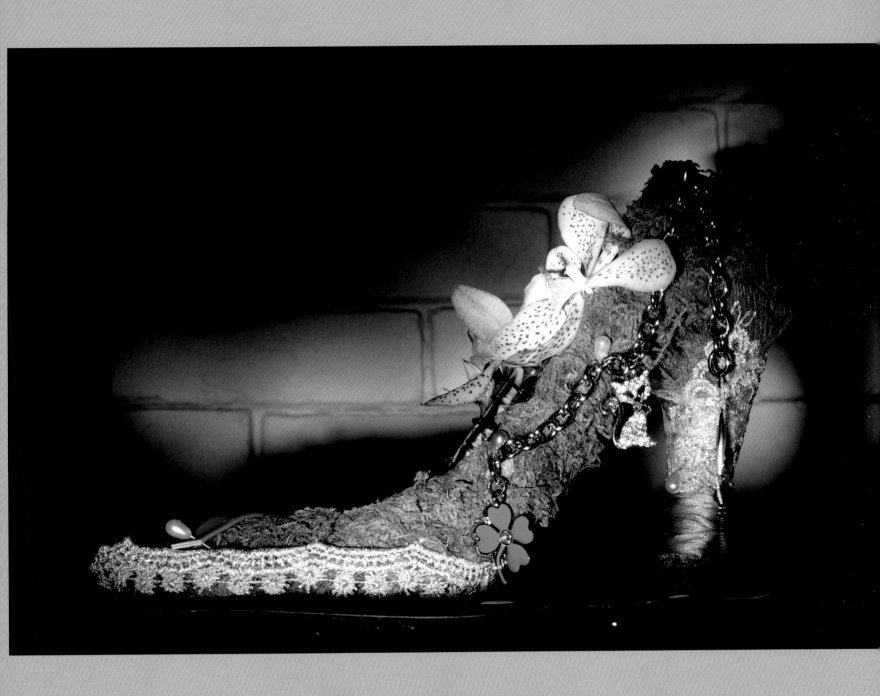

Roman ZARUBIN
Russia

Roman ZARUBIN
Russia

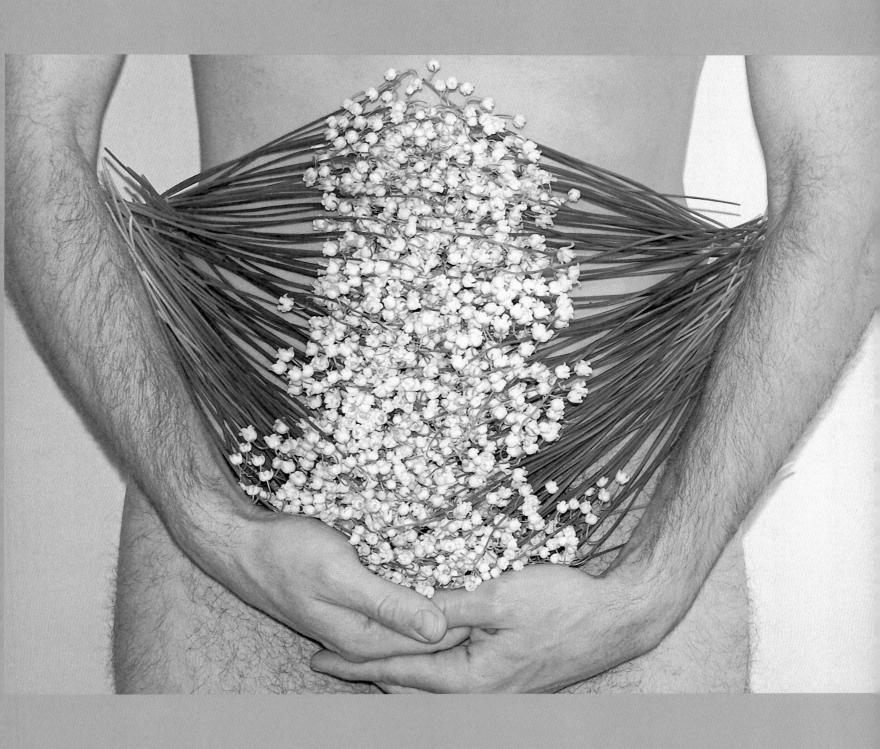

Natalia ZHIZHKO
Russia

Irina ZHIGALOVA
Russia

ARTISTS

06/07

Jean-Louis AMICE
France

p. 34: Celosia bombay, Clematis
p. 35: Phytolacca, Hydrangea, Sambucus nigra, Cellosia, Viburnum, Ammi majus
Photography: Cédric Prat

p. 34-35

Roseanne ARMSTRONG
New Zealand

p. 37: Lilium (that had mutated while growing), Allium, Cannamois virgata
Photography: Melinda Baigent

p. 37

Ingeborg AUGUSTUS
Belgium

p. 36: Lunaria annua, Quercus ilex, Gypsophila elegans, Black eyed beans, Hortensia, Agave, Fregola discs
Photography: André Mathyssens & I. De Cuyper (portrait)

p. 36

Will BECKERS
The Netherlands

p. 38: Pennisetum grass, Rosa 'Virginia Red', Bronze nails, Natural wax, Jute, Raffia
p. 39: Asparagus setaceus, Clematis (flower), Phormium tenax variegata, Salix
p. 40-41: Jute, Natural wax, Graminaceae, Passiflora (flower)
Photography: Will Beckers

p. 38-41

Llum BENEDICTO ALONSO
Spain

p. 42: Gypsophila 'Million Star', Caspenia, Zinnia, Ceropegia
p. 43: Zinnia, Muehlenbeckia complexa
Photography: Frances Guillamet

p. 42-43

Per BENJAMIN
Sweden

p. 44-45: Gomphrena globosa, Sandersonia, Gloriosa rothschildiana, Nerine, Phalaenopsis
Photography: Helén Pe

p. 44-45

Alexander BERMIJAKOV
Russia

p. 46: Hydrangea hortensis, Vanda 'Trevor', Ceropegia sandersonii, Convolvulus arvensis
Photography: Leonid Gerkus

p. 46

Montse BOLET I SOLER
Spain

p. 48: Phyllostachys aurea
p. 49: Phormium tenax
Photography: Toni Galitó

p. 48-49

Ludmila BONDARCHUK
Russia

p. 50: Berberis thunbergi 'Golden Ring'
p. 51: Acer platanoides
Photography: Boris Bendikov & Dmitry Livshits

p. 50-51

Sabine BOONE
Belgium

p. 47: Buxus sempervirens (roots), Euphorbia globosa, Rosa 'Eden'
Photography: Kurt Dekeyzer

p. 47

Gil BOYARD
France

p. 52: Passiflora caerulea, Rudbeckia purpurea, Cucumis
p. 53: Oxalis purpurea
Photography: Patrick Sordoillet

p. 52-53

Irene BROCKWELL
Australia

p. 54-55: Anthurium andreanum 'Midori', Gomphocarpus physocarpus, Phalaenopsis hybrid 'Formosa stripes', Xanthorrhoea australis, Zantedeschia 'Majestic Red', Asymmetrical cane triangles, Gold bullion wire
Photography: Vincent Long

p. 54-55

Alexey BULATOV
Russia

p. 56: Solanum tuberosum 'Blue Eyes', Lerchenfeldia flexuosa (roots), Acer platanoides (dried leaves), Nepenthes (dries leaves), Heliconia regalis, Cedrus atlantica
Photography: Dmitry Livshits

p. 56

Marina BULATOVA
Russia

p. 57: Acer saccharinum
Photography: Dmitry Livshits

p. 57

Lieve BUYSSE
Belgium

p. 58: Dianthus 'Ivonne', 'Prado', 'Tico Tico', 'Peachy Mombo', 'Grand Slam', 'Ivana Orange', Rosa 'Anna', 'Timeless', 'Esperance', 'Black Magic', 'Metallina', 'Terra Cotta', 'Spray Pepita', 'Spray Tiramisu', 'Spray Oleysia', 'Spray Rumbo', Gerbera 'Finola'
p. 59: Cambria 'Odonthoglossum pardinum', Ophiopogon (t-grass)
Photography: Norberta Janssens

p. 58-59

Lorna CAMPBELL
United Kingdom

p. 60: Rubus fruticosus, Crataegus monogyna, Senecio rowleyanus
Photography: Lorna Campbell

p. 60

Nico CANTERS
Belgium

p. 61: Ligustrum vulgare berry, Pennisetum alopecuroides 'Red Jewel'
p. 62: Rosa rugosa, Asclepias tuberosa fruit, Hydrangea macrophylla (petals), Passiflora caerulea
p. 63: Hydrangea macrophylla, Xerophyllum, Rosa 'Black Baccara', Rosa 'Grand Prix', Rosa 'Old Dutch'
Photography: Kurt Dekeyzer

p. 61-63

Antonuccio CARMELO
Italy

p. 64: Plumeria rubra var. acutifolia, Passiflora coccinea (branches), Salix matsudana 'Tortuosa', Rubus fruticosus, Syagrus romanzoffiana, Thevetia peruviana (fruit), Agave americana, Opuntia ficus - indica, Holmskiodia sanguinea 'Mandarin Blue', Tamarix gallica, Stenocarpus sinuatus
Photography: Giuseppina Lucchesi & Rosario Spoto

p. 64

Jacques CASTAGNÉ
France

p. 65: Drosera, Fresh water algae, Wheat germ
p. 66: Juncus, Agave (core)
p. 67: Ligustrum, Nicandra (Physaloides), Snaken, Chinese cane
p. 68-69: Litchi chinensis
Photography: Daniel Mettoudi

p. 65-69

Anna CHAYKOVSKAYA
Russia

p. 71: Calamatus rotang, Chamaenerion angustifolium, Hyacinthus 'Anna Mai', Campanula latifolia, Craspedia globosa
Photography: Alexey Popov

p. 71

Jacques COOLEN
Germany

p. 72: Gerbera hybrids, Rumohra adiantiformis, Rosa toscani, Panicum fountain, Hydrangea macrophylla Red Baron, Asparagus umbellatus, Celosia cristata, Salvia officinalis, Mentha piperita, Lavandula angustifolia, Amaranthus caudatus, Achimella mollis, Cotinus coggygria (leaf and flower), Viburnum opulus
p. 73: Rosa 'Abraham Darby', Malus pumila 'Jonagold', Malus domestica 'Granny Smith'

p. 72-73   **Photography:** Klaus Pütz

Gudrun COTTENIER
Belgium

p. 74: Lilium longiflorum, Catalpa legumes
p. 75: Gerbera mini
Photography: Isabelle Persyn

p. 74-75

Claire COWLING
United Kingdom

p. 76: Phalaenopsis, Cereopegia woodii, Symphoricarpus, Phormium tenax, Eucalyptus berries, Lunaria annua, Carnation, Rose, Alocasia, Ampelopsis brevipedunculata
p. 77: Rose, Chrysanthemum, Malus, Physalis, Carnation, Panicum, Gingko, Capsicum, Passiflora, Xanthorrhoea australis, Phormium tenax, Corylus, Acer
p. 78: Lilium Longiflorum, Phalaenopsis, Cereopegia woodii, Symphoricarpus, Phormium tenax, Eucalyptus berries, Xanthorrhoea australis, Phyllostachys nigra, Various dried materials – pods, Strelitzia leaves, Feathers
Photography: Bruce Head

p. 76-78

Stijn CUVELIER
Belgium

p. 79: Phalaenopsis, Aspidistra leaf, Veneer wood beech
Photography: Kurt Dekeyzer

p. 79

Tomas DE BRUYNE
Belgium

p. 80: Pandanus amaryllifolius, Phalaenopsis hybrida, Smilax aspera
p. 81: Phalaenopsis hybrida, Darlingtonia California leaves
Photography: Kurt Dekeyzer

p. 80-81

Johanna DE CARNÉE
Germany

p. 82: Betula papyrifera
p. 83: Acer pseudoplatanus 'Atropurpureum'
Photography: Johanne de Carnée & Stefan Mertenskötter (portrait)

p. 82-83

Maria DE LA LUZ REYES CAMACHO
Spain

p. 70: Anthurium andreanum, Ceropegia Fusca
Photography: Teyo Bermejo

p. 70

André DEGRAER
Belgium

p. 87: Arundinaria gigantea (River cane), Lemna minor
Photography: Musschoot

p. 87

Kristof DE WAELE
Belgium

p. 84: Chrysanthemum, Adiantum venustum
p. 85: Chrysanthemum, Cinnamomum
p. 86: Cotinus, Viburnum
Photography: Joris Luyten

p. 84-86

André DIERICKX
Belgium

p. 88: Leycesteria formosa
p. 89: Salix, Vanda 'Dark Blue Magic'
p. 90: Viburnum opulus
p. 91: Phalaenopsis, Pulp cane
Photography: Kurt Dekeyzer

p. 88-91

Hilde ERLBACHER
Germany

p. 92: Adansonia digitata, Euphorbia spinosa, Brassolaelioca Aleya 'Golden Million', Gyptocerus anthonyanus
Photography: Helmut Bauer

p. 92

Birgit FARWICK
Germany

p. 94: Platycerium bifurcatum
p. 95: Cambria, Muehlenbeckia atillaris
Photography: Armin Knorreck

p. 94-95

Gislinde FOLKERTS
New Zealand

p. 93: Zantedeschia aethiopica 'Elfin', Dianthus, Asparagus plumosus, Bambusa, Coconut fibre
Photography: Tim Hawkins

p. 93

Araik GALSTYAN
Armenia

p. 96: Equisetum, Alisma plantago-aquatica
p. 97: Hydrangea macrophylla, Lemna trisulca, Lemna minor
Photography: Tatiana Liberman

p. 96-97

Lien GELLYNCK
Belgium

p. 98: Lunaria
p. 99: Stachys byzantina leaves, Hydrangea, Rosa, Tillandsia usneoides, Bruniaceae laevis
Photography: Geert Ver Eecke

p. 98-99

Richard GO
Australia

p. 100: Eucalyptus leucoxylon 'Rosea', Senecio radicans, Salix babylonica
Photography: Kym Thomson

p. 100

Sergio GONZALEZ
Spain

p. 101: Zantedeschia rehmanhii, Ornithogalum arabicum, Aranjia seriafera
p. 102: Ornithogalum arabicum, Asclepias Beatrix, Hypericum 'Sunny Classic', Chrysanthemum 'Yoko Ono', Nertera granadensis, Clematis vitalba, Ipomoea purpurea, Typha latifolia, Rosa hybrid
p. 103: Dendrobium 'Macora panee', Nertera granadensis, Pinus pinea, Lentisus minor, Ipomoea purpurea
Photography: Guillem Urbà

p. 101-103

Rita GYBELS
Belgium

p. 104-105: Hydrangea, Juniperus communis berries, Wisteria branch
p. 106: Gleditsia pods, Tropisia leaf
p. 107: Papaver, Capsicum annuum
Photography: Bart Van Leuven

p. 104-107

Karin HERGEMÖLLER
Germany

p. 108: Rosa 'Artemis'
p. 109: Viburnum lantana
Photography: Andre Adolph

p. 108-109

Marie & Peter HESS-BOSON
Switzerland

p. 110: Davallia mariesii, Davalliacea
p. 111: Bryophyllum daïgremontianum, Crassulacea
Photography: Werner Beetschen

p. 110-111

Allysha HUETER
Australia

p. 160: Draceana Draco foliage, Philodendron foliage
Photography: Markus Hueter

p. 160

Mit INGELAERE-BRANDT
Belgium

p. 113: Xerophyllum, Agave, Dahlia
Photography: Anika Ingelaere

p. 113

Kerstin JÖHREN
Germany

p. 114: Fagus sylvatica, Cyclamen haderi Jolium
p. 115: Rosa omeiensis
Photography: Caro Fetzer

p. 114-115

Annemie KANTERS-BEELEN
The Netherlands

p. 112: Haurus, Vine frame
Photography: Marga Nieboer

p. 112

Sergey KARPUNIN
Russia

p. 116: Gleichenia polypodioides (coral-fern), Kalanchoe blossfeldiana
p. 117: Delphinium 'Harlecijn', Delphinium 'Yvonne'
Photography: Victor & Natalia Smirnow

p. 116-117

Wally KLETT
Germany

p. 118: Rosa 'Esperanza', Ixora 'Kontiki', Peperomia caperata, Hedera
p. 119: Dendrobium, Vanda hybr., Muscari latifolium, Ripsalis var., Peperomia caperata, Asparagus scandens
Photography: Martin Fehrle

p. 118-119

Sabine KLOOSTERMAN-CALAME
Canada

p. 120: Dendrobium, Aspidistra elatior, Aristea confusa (Typha), Hypericum 'Autumn Blaze', Shells
Photography: Michelle Ingram

p. 120

Robert KOENE
Greece

p. 121: Ficinea fascicularis, Oncidium spacelatum, Schoenus melanostachys (Flexi grass)
p. 122: Vanda 'Red Magic', Xanthorrhea australis (Steel grass), Aristea confusa (Typha leaves), Asparagus asparagoides myrtifolius 'Smilax', Birch sheets, Panicum Fountain, Hydrangea macropylla
p. 123: Cymbidium
Photography: D. Lambropoulou Publishing EPE, EDHL (p. 127)
Vivianne Athanasopoulou (p. 128 & 129)

p. 121-123

Patrick KOKINOPOULOS
France

p. 124: Vanda, Raffia
p. 125: Xerophyllum, Piments, Morus leaves and fruit, Rose hips
Photography: Olivier Siddi

p. 124-125

Larisa KORKUNOVA
Russia

p. 127: Sphagnum, Viola x wittrockiana, Majanthemum bifolium, Aquilegia hybr., Atragene sibirica, Zinnia elegans, Oxalis valdiviensis, Geranium sylvaticum
Photography: Alexey Popov

p. 127

Thea KORNHERR
Germany

p. 128: Bulbine frutescens, Centaurea jacea, Cosmos bipinnatus, Cuphea, Diascia vigilis, Fagus sylvatica, Foeniculum vulgare, Galium sylvaticum, Geranium pratense, Heuchera hybrids, Knautia sylvatica, Miscanthus sinensis, Nermesia hybrids, Polygonum bistorta, Phlox paniculata, Rosa canina, Salvia, Sanguisorba officinalis, Solanum jaminoides, Trifolium medium
p. 129: Euonymus europaea, Fagus sylvatica, Fragaria, Petunia hybrids, Rosa, Rosa canina, Tagetes patula, Tropaeolum majus
Photography: Martin Kornherr

p. 128-129

Natalia KORYAKINA
Russia

p. 130: Chamaenerium angustifolium, Musa velutina
p. 131: Tussilago farfara, Amelanchier rotundifolia (berries), Rosa
p. 132-133: Araucaria geterophylla
Photography: Georgy Shablovsky

p. 130-133

Rotislav KRAVCHUK
Ukraine

p. 134: Malus x domestica, Ribes sylvestre 'Red Lake', Phalaenopsis hyb.
p. 135: Viburnum lantana
Photography: Juri Tschenerow

p. 134-135

Elena KUPRINA
Russia

p. 126: Nerine 'Stefanie', Jasminum polyanthum, Grasko
Photography: Victor & Natalia Smirnov

p. 126

Lowdi KWAN
Hongkong

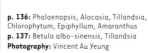

p. 136: Phalaenopsis, Alocasia, Tillandsia, Chlorophytum, Epiphyllum, Amaranthus
p. 137: Betula albo-sinensis, Tillandsia
Photography: Vincent Au Yeung

p. 136-137

Sofie LANNOY
Belgium

p. 148: Chrystanthemum santini (green and pink), Menta socka, Nigella damascena, Grasses, Tillandsia
Photography: Isabelle Persyn

p. 148

Madeleine LAST
The Netherlands

p. 138: Cirsium vulgare, Gossypium
Photography: Marieke Korver & Ben R. Verwijs (portrait)

p. 138

Konstantin LAZAREV
Russia

p. 140: Tanacetum officinalis, Echinacea purpurea
p. 141: Tanacetum officinalis, Crataegus sanguinea, Echinacea purpurea
Photography: Vladimir Smolentsev

p. 140-141

Arnaud LECHANTRE
France

p. 146: Rose hips
p. 147: White leaves, Tillandsia
Photography: Jean-Pierre Mainury

p. 146-147

Muriel LE COULS
France

p. 142: Gousse d'Entada, Actinidia, Lathyrus, Crocosmia
p. 143: Juncus, Capsicum
p. 144: Coffea arabica, Catalpa bignonioïdes, Rudbeckia 'Herbstsonne', Ceropegia, Ribes nigrum
p. 145: Scabiosa stellata, Piper, Cissus radix
Photography: Patrick Sordoillet

p. 142-145

Anne LEESON
Canada

p. 139: White Mitsumata branches, Helleborus x hybridus 'Anemone Dark', Zantedeschia, Senecio Herranus
Photography: Martin Schwalbe

p. 139

Uta LORENZ
Germany

p. 152: Craspedia globosa, Cardiospermum halicacabum, Scabiosa caucasica, Masdevallia candata, Gloriosa superba
Photography: Jörg Manegold

p. 152

Anson LOW
Singapore

p. 149: Dendrobium, Orchid root
p. 150: Gloriosa rothschildiana, Rosa, Cymbidium, Hydrangea, Smilax, Black Bean, Dischidia, Rhipsalis cassutha, Carthamus tinctorus stem
p. 151: Vanda Orchid, Dendrobium Orchid leaf, Carthamus tinctorus stem
Photography: Matthew Tan

p. 149-151

Hanneke MAASSEN
The Netherlands

p. 153: Papaver somniferum, Viburnum, Stephanotis floribunda, Rosa 'Rumba', Clematis alpina, Rhipsalis
Photography: Gerhard van Roon

p. 153

Sergei Vladimirovich MALYUCHENKO
Russia

p. 154: Malus, Clematis
p. 155: Buplearum sticks, Hedychium flowers
Photography: Andrei Kuznetsov

p. 154-155

Svetlana METALNIKOVA
Russia

p. 156: Sphagnum, Festuca pratensis, Picea obovata
p. 157: Sphagnum, Vaccinium vitis-idaea, Arctium lappa, Betula pubescens, Humulus lupulus, Anemone sylvestris, Cypripedium guttatum
p. 158: Ranunculus, Viola x wittrockiana, Rosa 'Cézanne', Eustoma russellianum 'Mariachi Misty Blue', Phaseolus coccineus
Photography: Alexey Popov

p. 156-158

Jasja MIDDELBEEK-VAN DER WAAL
The Netherlands

p. 159: Rosa 'Revue'
Photography: Kees Stuip

p. 159

Sandra MÖLLER
Germany

p. 161: Scabiosa stellata, Echinacea purpurea, Lathyrus latifolius, Dahlia hybrids, Calendula officinalis, Clematis, Pelargonium, Passiflora caerulea, Thunbergia alata, Tropaeolum majus, Cardiospermum halicacabum, Scabiosa atropurpurea, Salvia viridis, Fragaria
Photography: Bart Van Leuven

p. 161

Holly MONEY-COLLINS
USA

p. 162: Osa, Dianthus, Erica gracilis, Chrysanthemum, Viburnum, Pimelea, Brunia, Cladonia rangiferina, Gaultheria shallon, Salix babylonica
Photography: Derek Rothchild

p. 162

Richard MOS
The Netherlands

p. 163: Peeled Salix, Ophiopogon, Eleogaris acicularis, Typha latifolia, Jute
Photography: Yolanda Hart & Patrick Spaander (portrait)

p. 163

Guido MÜSKENS
The Netherlands

p. 164: Salix alba 'Chermesina'
p. 165: Equisetum hyemale
Photography: Foto Verbeeten

p. 164-165

JURY

Montse NADAL MESTRES
Spain

p. 166: Triticum, Stipa tenacissima
Photography: Eva Barceló Melgarejo

p. 166

Dorle NIELSEN
Germany

p. 167: Lamina riales
Photography: David Elmer

p. 167

Yukiko NISHIMURA
Japan

p. 168: Dicranopteris Linearis, Mokara chark kwan farn, Stemona japonica, Chrysanthemum
p. 169: Parthenocissus sugarvine, Mokara yipsum orange, Eustoma grandiflorum, Hydrangea macrophylla, Dicranopteris Linearis
Photography: Sachiko Onishi

p. 168-169

Hiroyuki OKA
Japan

p. 170: Clematis florida, Sorbus gracilis, Phyllostachys bambusoides
p. 171: Scabiosa atropurpurea, Allium ceps.
p. 172: Phragmipedium besseae, Capsicum annuum
p. 173: Citrus aurantium, Celastrus orbiculatus
Photography: Kiyokazu Nakashima

p. 170-173

Erika OLDENHOF
The Netherlands

p. 174: Lotyledon undulata, Kalanchoe blossfeldiana 'Calandiva', Ceropegia linearis ssp Woodii
p. 175: Paphiopedilum
Photography: Ger van Leeuwen

p. 174-175

Emilia OLIVERIO
France

p. 176: Sempervirum, Beans of the tulip tree, Sambucus nigra berries, Pinus
p. 177: Sempervirum, Oncidium, Nutans
p. 178: Eucalyptus sunny, Senecio Articulata Kleinia
Photography: John Henry Walzl

p. 176-178

Mark PAMPLING
Australia

p. 182: Ficus roxburghii, Philodendron scandens, Phalaenopsis 'Formosa Stripes', Zantedeschia 'Majestic Red', Sanseveria cylindrical, Nolina recurvata
p. 183: Xanthorrhoea australis, Aspidistra elatior, Phalaenopsis 'Bonnie Versque', Liriope muscari
Photography: Vincent Long

p. 182-183

Salvatore PAPARELLA
Italy

p. 184: Lycopersicon esculentum, Capsicum annum, Musa paradisiaca
p. 185: Phytolacca decandra, Sambucus nigra, Mahonia aquifolium, Diospyros kaki, Equisetum, Parthenocissus quinquefolia, Ampelopsis tricuspidata, Sedum, Hedera helix
Photography: Giuliano Barbuto

p. 184-185

Jin-Young PARK
Korea

p. 179: Celosia cristata, Micado stick
p. 180: Aspidistra, Hydrangea, Smilax china, Jasminum line, Wisteria line
p. 181: Epironia articulata, Oxypetalum caeruleum, Smilax china
Photography: Koo Ja Ick

p. 179-181

Karin PASMAN
The Netherlands

p. 187: Gerbera 'Rosta' , Clathrus
Photography: Jan de Koning & Andre van den Bos (portrait)

p. 187

Geert PATTYN
Belgium

p. 188-189: Xerophyllum (Beargrass)
p. 190: Aspidistra, Paeonia 'Dr. Flemming'
p. 191: Salix
Photography: Bart Van Leuven

p. 188-191

Inna PETRENKO
Ukraine

p. 186: Hidranhema, Phalaenopsis, Xerophyllum
Photography: Petrenko I.

p. 186

Rob PLATTEL
The Netherlands

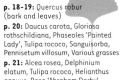

p. 18-19: Quercus robur (bark and leaves)
p. 20: Daucus carota, Gloriosa rothschildiana, Phaseoles 'Painted Lady', Tulipa rococo, Sanguisorba, Pennisetum villosum, Various grasses
p. 21: Alcea rosea, Delphinium elatum, Tulipa rococo, Helianthus annuus, Rosa 'Abraham Darby', Calendula officinalis, Lilium 'Pink Perfection', Papaver somniferum, Tropaeolum majus, Tagetes patula, Dahlia, Lathyrus, Campsis radicans, Viola Wittrockiana, Phlox paniculata, Centaurea Montana, Lupinus polyphyllus, Fuchsia, Cynara cardunculus, Vitis vinifera, Hemerocallis
p. 22-23: Polygonum ribrum, Sorbus aucuparia, Viburnum opulus, Sambucus nigra, Rhamnus, Mahonia japonica
Photography: Chris van Koeverden

p. 16-23

SILVER LEAF

Kristel REMIJN
The Netherlands

p. 192: Tulipa
Photography: Sandra van As

p. 192

Stefan ROOSEN
Belgium

p. 193: Sikkam fruit, Maclura fruit, Peppercorns (green and pink)
p. 194: Madeira wood, Sikkam fruit, Clematis vitalba
p. 195: Malus, Paraffin
Photography: Joris Luyten

p. 193-195

Veaceslav ROSCA
Russia

p. 196: Heracleum mantegazzianum, Kniphofia 'Alcazar', Celosia 'Bombay Red', Alstroemeria 'Valencia', Eremurus, Moluccella
p. 197: Xerophyllum, Phalaenopsis, Dianthus 'Prado', Scindapsus
Photography: Vladimir E. Kalinin

p. 196-197

Valérie J. ROY
Australia

p. 198-199: Eucalyptus caesia ssp caesia (Bark), Stephanotis floribunda, Helleborus x hybridus
Photography: Peter Hasson

p. 198-199

Mieko SAKAGUCHI
Japan

p. 200: Helianthus, Dahlia, Scabiosa, Astrantia, Foeniculum, Justicia brandegeeana, Sorbus commixta, Echinacea purpurea
Photography: Joji Okamoto

p. 200

Naoki SASAKI
Japan

p. 201: Corylopsis spicata
p. 202-203: Red leaves, Grass, Bambusa
p. 204: Lilium japonicum platyfolium, Aspidistra
p. 205: Cosmos, Japanese Enkianthus, Paederia scandens
Photography: Teruo Sasaki

p. 201-205

Ute SCHMIDT
Germany

p. 206: Viola, Stachys, Clematis, Senecio, Sempervivium, Akelei, Heuchera, Sedum, Ribes rubrum, Platanus, Hosta, Rudbeckia, Fagus sylvatica, Rosa, Beans
Photography: Barbara Rötzer

p. 206

Anja SCHNEIDER
Germany

p. 207: Fagus sylvatica, Zantedeschia elliottiana, Phalaenopsis cultivar, Anthurium audracanium, Prunus spinosa, Kalanchoe beharensis
Photography: Andreas Faber & Johanne de Carnée (portrait)

p. 207

Zhanna SEMENOVA
Russia

BRONZE LEAF

p. 24: Ammi visnaga 'Green Mist'
p. 26-27: Tritelia 'Corina', Macaroni
p. 28-29: Euphorbia fulgens 'Quicksilver'
p. 30-31: Mini bamboo cane, Cardo, Sea grass
Photography: Valentin E. Overchenko

p. 24-31

Jouni SEPPÄNEN
Finland

JURY

p. 208-209: Convallaria majalis, Rosa 'Grandiflora', Syringa vulgaris 'Madame Florent Stepman', Viburnum opulus 'Roseum'
p. 210-211: Convallaria majalis, Syringa vulgaris 'Madame Florent Stepman', Viburnum opulus 'Roseum'
Photography: Nina Kellokoski & Katja Lösönen (portrait)

p. 208-211

Sveta SHVEDENKOVA
Russia

p. 212: Acryl, Shells, Paper, Gold foil, Pins, Skeletonised leaves
p. 213: Phaseolus, Mushrooms
Photography: Sveta Shvedenkova

p. 212-213

Giordano SIMONELLI
Italy

p. 214: Juncus, Anthurium 'Deep Purple', Zantedeschia elliottiana
Photography: Benito Vanicelli

p. 214

Alla SOKOLOVA
Russia

p. 215: Rosa, Sorghum
Photography: G. Shablovsky

p. 215

Alexander SPEK
The Netherlands

p. 216: Vanda, Anthurium, pods from Laos
p. 217: Gloriosa
Photography: Marc Vreenegoor

p. 216-217

Britta SPELLEKEN
Germany

p. 218: Pinus nigra Pinaceae
Photography: Christoph Düpper

p. 218

Ulrich STELZER
Germany

p. 220: Phalaenopsis, Miltonia, Cambria, Cattleya, Paphiopedilum, Cyclamen, Kalanchoe, Anthurium, Calla, Rosa, Cineraria, Fragaria, Physalis, Gloriosa, Carex, Lilium, Citrus, Ardisia
p. 221: Rosa, Cosmea, Viola, Geranium, Lunaria, Clematis, Beans, Lonicera, Allium, Salix, Ribes rubrum, Rubus idaeus, Ipomoea, Aquilegia, Begonia semperflorens
Photography: Barbara Rötzer

p. 220-221

Iain STEPHENS
New Zealand

p. 219: Cane, Agar (Chinese noodles), Philodendron leaves, Strelitzia juncea (spear grass)
Photography: Vicky Broadbent

p. 219

Frida SVENINGSSON
Sweden

p. 222-223: Hyacinthus orientalis
Photography: Christian Karnevald

p. 222-223

Yuko TADAMURA
Japan

p. 224: Clematis patens 'Hakuba', Smilax, Hydrangea arborescens, Tussilago farfara
p. 225: Clematis integrifolia 'Rooguchi', Helichrysum, Tussilago farfara
Photography: Takashi Anamizu

p. 224-225

Yuko TAKAGI
Japan

GOLDEN LEAF

p. 10-11: Vigna radiata, Phalaenopsis, Rivina humilis, Maxillaria tenuifolia
p. 12: Nelumbo nucifera, Capsicum annuum, Chrysanthemum morifolium
p. 13: Clematis hybrida
p. 14-15: Vigna radiata, Vanda, Mokara, Smilax aspera, Capsicum annuum, Rubus spp, Ceropegia liearis subsp. Woodii, Eucalyptus tetoragona, Hydrangea, Echeveria
Photography: Satoshi Shiozaki

p. 8-15

June TAN
Singapore

p. 226: Zantedeschia rehmannii, Black Beans, Dischidia Roots, Seeded Eucalyptus
p. 227: Red dates, Black fungus, Smilax, Reindeer Moss
Photography: Matthew Tan

p. 226-227

Tracy TOMLINSON
United Kingdom

p. 228: Verbena bonariensis, Buddleja Davidii, Astilbe cattleya, Cosmos 'Black Beauty', Miscanthus, Penstemon, Typha, Origanum
p. 229: Angelica gigas, Vitas vinifera
Photography: Frank Tomlinson

p. 228-229

Irine TRENYOVA
Russia

p. 230-231: Ornithogalum saundersiae
Photography: Victor & Natalia Smirnow

p. 230-231

Tatjana TRIDVORNOVA
Estonia

p. 232: Tropaeolum majus
Photography: Sergei Maslow

p. 232

Chris TRULLEMANS
Belgium

p. 233: Platycerium, Disa orchidaceae
Photography: Steven Van Leeuw

p. 233

Teresa Maria Ineke TURANGAN
Indonesia

p. 234: Leucaena glauca, Limonium, Gomphrena globosa
p. 235: Heliconia psittacorum
p. 236: Cocos nucifera, Asclepias physocarpa, Jasminum sambac
Photography: Ruby Chrissandy

p. 234-236

Riou UDAGAWA
Japan

p. 237: Cryptomeria Japonica, Prunus jamasakura, Pinus parviflora, Celastrus orbiculatus, Japanese cedar board, Mallet, Snow shoes, Lid of iron pod
Photography: Kenichi Ogoshi & Shigeru Tanaka (portrait)

p. 237

Andy Djati UTOMO
Indonesia

p. 238: Brunia lanuginosa, Cordyline terminalis, Hypericum, Aranthera 'James Story', Eucalyptus
p. 239: Phalaenopsis hybr., Ornithogalum arabicum, Brunia lanuginosa
p. 240: Xanthorrhoea tenax, Ornithogalum dubium, Sambucus nigra, Echinacea purpurea, Brunia lanuginosa, Craspedia globosa
p. 241: Dendrobium hybr., Ornithogalum thrysoides, Brunia albiflora
Photography: Ruby Chrissandy

p. 238-241

Mark VAN BERCKELAER
France

p. 242-243: Platanus (bark), Orchis (roots), Viburnum betulifolium, Pepper
p. 244: Vanda coerulea, Leucocoryne ixioides, Rubus fruticosus, Flexi Grass, Pepper
p. 245: Ceropegia, Heliconia, Salix, Platanus (bark), Orchis (roots), Viburnum betulifolium
Photography: Christian Offroy

p. 242-245

Moniek VANDEN BERGHE
Belgium

p. 246-247: Seaweed, Vanda blue magic, Vanda dark blue magic
p. 248: Zantedeschia 'Pink Persuasion', Rodochiton
p. 249: Stachys bysantina, Phalaenopsis 'Black Eagle', Ferns
Photography: Kurt Dekeyzer

p. 246-249

Carl VANDERMOERE
Belgium

p. 250: Vaccinium macrocarpon, Moss, Poncirus trifoliata
p. 251: Ilex verticillata, Tillandsia, Poncirus trifoliata, Vanda
Photography: Joris Luyten & Bart Van Leuven (portrait)

p. 250-251

Marion VAN DER VEEN
The Netherlands

p. 252: Clematis vitalba, Clematis montana
p. 253: Hydrangea macrophylla, Hydrangea macrophylla bleached, Narcissus 'Tête à tête', Delphinium ajacis, Rosa 'Valentino', Transparant foil
p. 254: Bromus tectorum, Rice paper
p. 255: Lunaria annua, Paeonia officinalis
Photography: Corrie de Kruif

p. 252-255

Max VAN DE SLUIS
The Netherlands

p. 256: Eggshell of an ostrichegg, moss, Muscari
p. 257: Slate, moss, Narcissus tazetta
Photography: Pim van der Maden

p. 256-257

Marcel VAN DIJK
The Netherlands

p. 258-259: Gloriosa Rothschildiana
p. 260-261: Agave americana
Photography: Bart Van Leuven

p. 258-261

Herman VAN DIONANT
Belgium

p. 262: Equisetum, Oncidium
p. 263: Phalaenopsis, Cotinus, Tillia
Photography: Kurt Dekeyzer

p. 262-263

Françoise VANDONINK
Belgium

p. 264: Tillandsia xerographica, Hydrangea macrophylla, Pulp cane, Peppercorns
p. 265: Agave, Phalaenopsis 'Ravel Chuck's', Phalaenopsis 'Master', Phalaenopsis 'Salmon Dream', Phalaenopsis 'Medar Spots', Phalaenopsis 'Red Oconee', Phalaenopsis 'Ever Spring Pioneer Champion', Vanda 'Blue Magic', Datura fruit
Photography: Joris Luyten

p. 264-265

Annick VAN WESEMAEL
Belgium

p. 266-267: Waxflower 'Wendy', Calla 'Captain Rosette', Calla 'Captain Romance', Agave transparent burgundy, Rose petals
p. 268: Muscari botryoides
p. 269: Convalaria majalis
Photography: Joris Luyten

p. 266-269

Charlotte VÖGELE
Germany

p. 270: Picea abies, Betula utilis
p. 271: Rosa canina
Photography: Christian Döge (p. 278), Rainer Lehmann (p. 279) & Edith Strupf (portrait)

p. 270-271

Kristin VORELAND
Norway

p. 272: Hypericum green, Panicum, Hand-made paper
p. 273: Prunus maacii, Rhammus catharticus, Ribes aureum, Aronia mitscurinii 'Viking'
Photography: Pål Hoff

p. 272-273

Jessica WAHL
Sweden

p. 274: Pinus sylvestris, Sedum spectabilis 'Matrona', Anemone hupehensis
p. 275: Pinus sylvestris, Stachys byzantina, Lilium x hollandicum 'Vermeer', Ribes rubrum, Haworthia attenuate, Ceropegia woodii, Cotinus coggygria
p. 276-277: Astilbe arendsii, Chrysanthemum x grandiflorum (santini) 'Jeanny Salmon', Sedum 'Postman's Pride', Cotinus coggygria, Acer palmatum 'Atropurpureum', Kalanchoë x blossfeldiana, Viburnum opulus, Rubus fruticosus, Phalaenopsis
Photography: Morgan Norman

p. 274-277

Catharine WATSON
United Kingdom

p. 278: Pyrus salicifolia branches, Cymbidium
p. 279: Quercus branches
Photography: Paul Watson

p. 278-279

Neil WHITTAKER
United Kingdom

p. 280: Vanda 'Orange Magic', Typha leaf, Xerophyllum tenax
p. 281: Vanda 'Orange Magic', Rhipsalis, Beads
Photography: Dennis Bradley & Neil Whittaker

p. 280-281

Charlotte YUEN
Hongkong

p. 283: Orchids, Moss
Photography: Sonny

p. 283

Jörg ZABEL
Germany

p. 282: Protea 'Blushing Bride', Rosa 'Abraham Darby', Symphoricarpos rosa, Agapanthus africanus, Asclepias, Zantedeschia aethiopica, Rosa 'Elisabeth', Heuchera americana
Photography: Monika Wernecke

p. 282

Roman ZARUBIN
Russia

p. 284: Stachys byzantina, Eringium planum
p. 285: Acer platanoides
p. 286: Calamaglostis epigeios
Photography: Boris Bendikov

p. 284-286

Irina ZHIGALOVA
Russia

p. 290: Asclepias siriaca, Nigella damascena, Delphinium elatum
p. 291: Physalis alkekengi
Photography: Tatiana Liberman

p. 290-291

Natalia ZHIZHKO
Russia

p. 288: Pinus sylvestris, Pinus pinaster, Sorbus aucuparia, Rosa 'Mary Clear'
p. 289: Fraxinus excelsior, Cosmos bipinnatus
Photography: Lukin Alexei

p. 288-289

Stanislav ZUBOV
Russia

p. 287: Convallaria majalis
Photography: Viacheslav Vergelesov

p. 287